CW00538141

WESTBURY
TO
BATH

Vic Mitchell and Keith Smith

MP Middleton Press

Cover picture: With the elegant Bath stone Barton Bridge in the foreground, no. 33004 crosses the River Avon at Bradford-on-Avon on 2nd April 1988. The train is the 12.10 from Portsmouth Harbour to Cardiff. The old bridge now only carries a footpath. (P.G.Barnes)

First published July 1995

ISBN 1 873793 55 3

© Middleton Press 1995

Design - Deborah Goodridge

Published by Middleton Press
   Easebourne Lane
   Midhurst
   West Sussex
   GU29 9AZ
   Tel: 01730 813169
   Fax: 01730 812601

Printed & bound by Biddles Ltd,
   Guildford and Kings Lynn

CONTENTS

ACKNOWLEDGEMENTS

In addition to those mentioned in the photographic credits, we would like to convey our gratitude for assistance received to W.R.Burton, D.Cullum, R.M.Casserley, G.Croughton, M.King, N.Langridge, Mr.D. & Dr. S. Salter, N.Sprinks, A.G.Thorpe and our ever supportive wives.

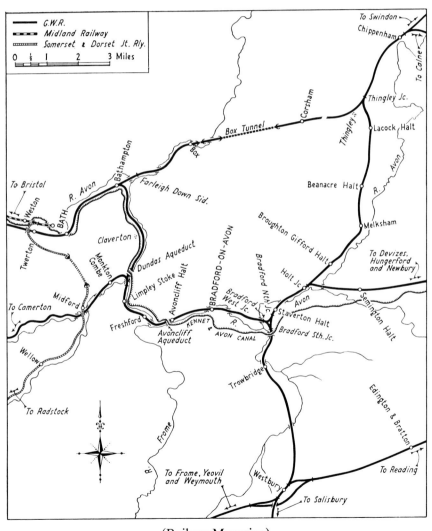

(Railway Magazine)

GEOGRAPHICAL SETTING

Westbury is an old-established market town situated at the foot of the chalk downs of Salisbury Plain and close to the infant River Bliss. The line runs along its valley to Trowbridge and traverses predominantly Oxford Clay, although ironstone deposits occur in the vicinity of Westbury.

The route follows the River Avon closely from Bradford Junction to Bath, passing through the Avon Gap in the limestone mass of the southern extension of the Cotswold Hills. Bath stone has been quarried or, more commonly, mined in this area for centuries and has generated considerable rail traffic in the past.

The maps are to the scale of 25" to 1 mile, unless otherwise indicated.

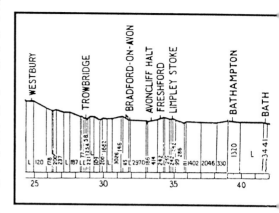

HISTORICAL BACKGROUND

The Great Western Railway's Bristol - Bath line opened on 31st August 1840 and was extended east through Box Tunnel to Chippenham on 30th June 1841. A branch running south-west from this section was opened to Westbury via Melksham on 5th September 1848, being part of the Wilts, Somerset and Westbury Railway (which was purchased by the GWR on 14th March 1850). It was extended to Frome in 1850 and to Warminster in 1851. All these routes were laid to the broad gauge of 7ft 0¼ins.

A single line between Bathampton and Trowbridge, through Bradford-on-Avon, came into use on 2nd February 1857. It was converted to standard gauge on 18-22 July 1874 and was doubled on 17th May 1885.

Later additions to the railway map of the area included -
Bradford West to North Junction 1895
Westbury eastwards 1900
Limpley Stoke to Camerton 1910
Westbury cut-off 1933

Subsequent closures have been few, these including the Camerton branch and the Bradford North to West Junction spur. The dates are given near the appropriate pictures.

PASSENGER SERVICES

The route has carried trains to a greater variety of destinations than most and so simple summaries are not possible. Common termination points have included Bristol, Cardiff, Swindon, Devizes, Salisbury, Southampton and Portsmouth. To illustrate this diversity of service, we quote some down (Westbury to Bath) weekday timetables for selected stations in various years, the train description being that published although it sometimes operated over a longer route.

Dieselisation in the mid-1960s brought only minor changes but the introduction of Sprinters in 1988 gave an increase in frequency. Further improvements in 1992 resulted in 26 trains each weekday on the Salisbury route in addition to nine on the Weymouth line, but the Melksham line had only one train each way, Monday - Friday only (between Frome and Swindon).

Bradford-upon-Avon
December 1870

am
7.45	Salisbury to Bath
8.22	Devizes to Bath

pm
12.5	Weymouth to Bristol
3.20	Weymouth to Bath
4.40	Devizes to Bath
8.15	Salisbury to Bristol

No Sunday trains

Trowbridge
July 1915

am
3.30	Portsmouth to Bristol
7.12	Westbury to Bath
8.6	Trowbridge to Bristol
8.36	Trowbridge to Bath
9.7	Salisbury to Bath
10.37	Salisbury to Bristol
11.6	Portsmouth to Cardiff
11.20	Reading to Bristol

pm
12.5	Trowbridge to Hallatrow
12.42	Reading to Bristol

2.0	Salisbury to Weston-super-Mare
2.41	Westbury to Bath
3.0	Trowbridge to Hallatrow
4.2	Portsmouth to Bristol
4.22	Westbury to Bristol
5.26	Portsmouth to Bristol
6.18	Trowbridge to Bath
6.35	Westbury to Bristol
7.56	Portsmouth to Cardiff
8.12	Trowbridge to Bristol
9.28	Westbury to Bristol

Trowbridge
September 1960

am
3.45	Salisbury to Bristol
6.42	Trowbridge to Bradford-upon-Avon
7.4	Westbury to Bristol
7.55	Westbury to Taunton
8.40	Salisbury to Bristol
9.53	Weymouth to Bristol
10.55	Westbury to Bristol
11.13	Salisbury to Bristol

pm
12.17	Portsmouth to Cardiff
12.46	Weymouth to Bristol

1.11	Salisbury to Bristol
1.53	Trowbridge to Bristol
2.21	Weymouth to Bristol
2.32	Brighton to Cardiff
2.57	Westbury to Bristol
3.45	Trowbridge to Bradford-upon-Avon
3.52	Weymouth to Bristol
4.25	Westbury to Bristol
5.12	Portsmouth to Bristol
5.27	Westbury to Bristol
6.17	Westbury to Bristol
6.37	Salisbury to Cardiff
6.48	Weymouth to Bristol
7.10	Weymouth to Bristol
7.23	Trowbridge to Bath
7.51	Westbury to Bristol
8.35	Portsmouth to Cardiff
9.24	Weymouth to Bristol
9.50	Trowbridge to Bristol
10.52	Westbury to Bath

Three other trains joined the route at Bradford West Junction, the times being shown at Bradford-upon-Avon.

9.4am	Chippenham to Bristol
5.9pm	Paddington to Weston-super-Mare via Devizes
5.43pm	Melksham to Bath

Bradshaw for November 1930 used the up and down
designations as applied to the Salisbury - Westbury section.

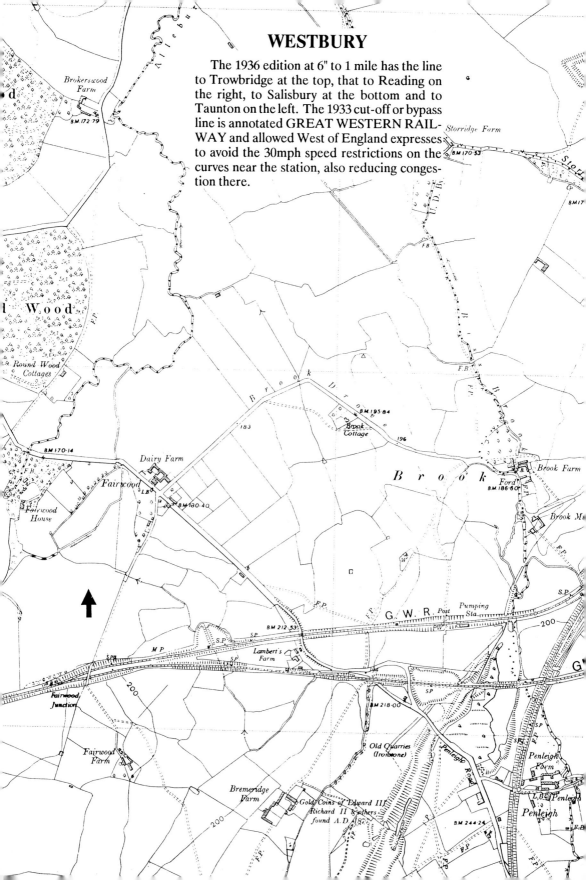

WESTBURY

The 1936 edition at 6" to 1 mile has the line to Trowbridge at the top, that to Reading on the right, to Salisbury at the bottom and to Taunton on the left. The 1933 cut-off or bypass line is annotated GREAT WESTERN RAILWAY and allowed West of England expresses to avoid the 30mph speed restrictions on the curves near the station, also reducing congestion there.

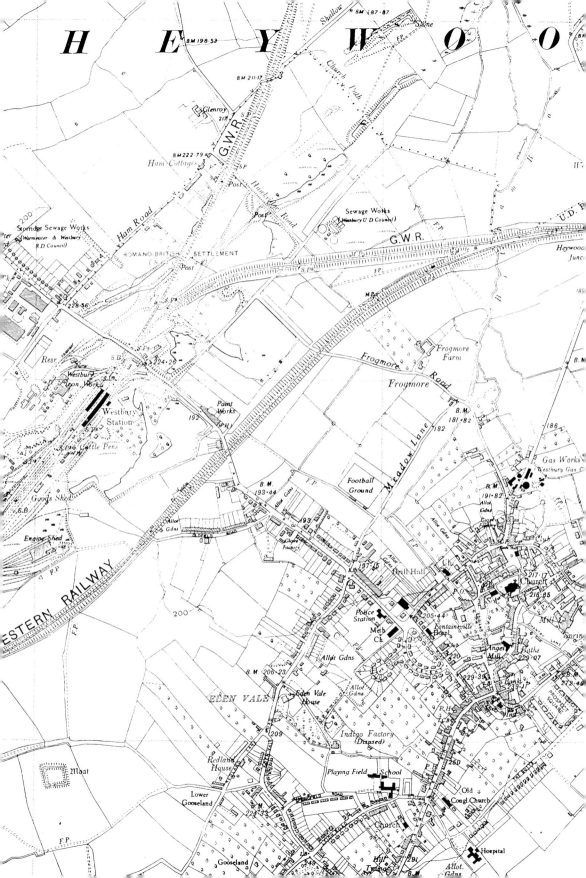

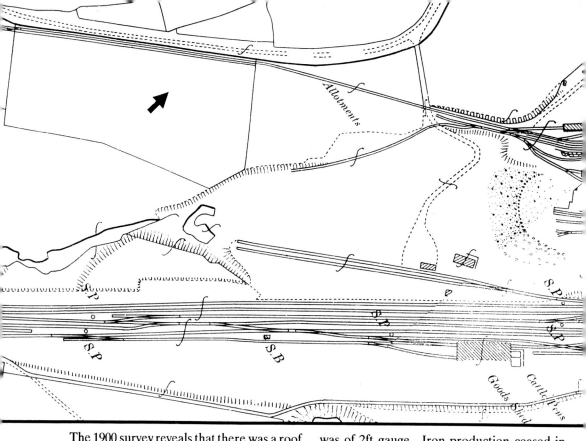

The 1900 survey reveals that there was a roof over the platforms and two through lines. The connection to the Westbury Iron Works site was maintained from 1870 until 1941. The ore was dug from a seam about 10ft thick and over one mile long. The work's tramway to the pits was of 2ft gauge. Iron production ceased in 1908, most of the coal required having come from Somerset colleries. Up to 100 000 tons of ore were quarried in some years, this ceasing in 1923. The site has been used subsequently for various engineering purposes.

1. Westbury Iron Works and North Box are on the right of this view from the road bridge. The overall roof was demolished prior to the construction of two island platforms in 1899 in readiness for the opening of the direct line from Reading in 1900. (Lens of Sutton)

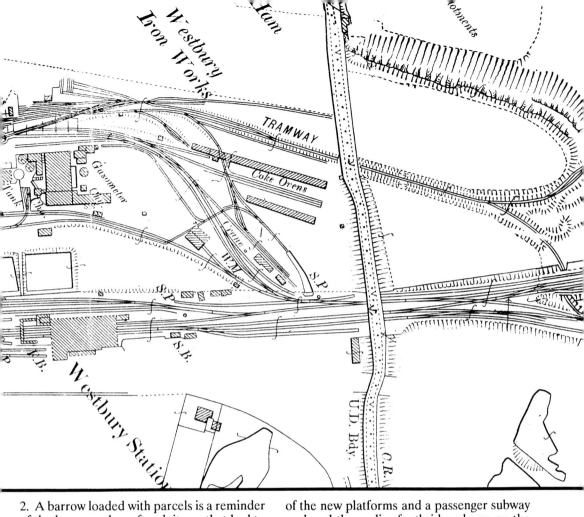

2. A barrow loaded with parcels is a reminder of the large number of such items that had to change trains here and that this was very labour intensive. Luggage lifts were provided on both of the new platforms and a passenger subway replaced the earlier footbridge shown on the map. (Lens of Sutton)

3. This is the down goods avoiding line which was brought into use in 1907; a similar line on the up side was completed in 1915. The photograph dates from 1921. The down reception line is now on this site. (H.C.Casserley coll.)

4. It is evident that the platform canopy was much longer on the down side than on the up. We witness two pannier tanks basking in the morning sun, the nearer one being at platform 1. Middle box was situated near the ramp and was in use until 5th May 1968. (Wessex coll.)

5. A DMU departs on the down main line on 13th July 1964. The down Salisbury line is in front of South Box (which closed on 19th September 1978), and the station is in the distance. Local goods facilities ceased on 1st November 1966. (R.C.Riley)

6. A panoramic view on 28th April 1982 shows no. 33038 waiting with the 06.56 Portsmouth - Bristol service, while, to its left, DMU set B811 forms the connecting Bristol - Weymouth working. At this time the north end of the station was still mechanically signalled, the south end colour lights being worked from a panel in the old north box. (G.Gillham)

7. No. 33062 passes the sole remaining signal box, hauling the 15.10 Portsmouth to Bristol on 17th August 1981. The box ceased to function while the station was completely closed for track remodelling from 7th April to 13th May 1984. During this period, platform 1 (left) was closed and the rails lifted. (D.Mitchell)

8. On 25th January 1990, storm force winds affected much of the UK and the canopy was severely damaged. Due to falling debris the station was closed to passengers. Trains on all four approach routes were halted at South or North Junctions soon after midday. After having stood for three hours, the trains were allowed forward, one by one, to the platform extremities away from the buildings, passengers then detraining and being led across tracks to take refuge in the nearby BR Training Centre - many not leaving until the following day. Viewed (with BR permission) from a part of the station least damaged, no. 155319 (which had been forming the 11.10 Portsmouth - Cardiff) stands after having discharged its passengers, whilst the 08.26 Penzance - Paddington HST (with power car 43026 *City of Westminster* leading) is subject to a similar process. (S.McMullin)

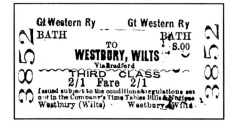

9. Westbury Yard has become the centre for the important stone traffic from both the Foster Yeoman Merehead Quarry and the ARC Whatley Quarry in the Mendips. Privately owned no. 59001 *Yeoman Endeavour* runs through with down empties on 24th November 1994. (M.J.Stretton)

10. Recorded on the same day was the yard shunter (no. 09102) and the offices bearing the new "Mainline" logo. There were 16 sidings on the down side and 17 on the up. One of the short sidings north-east of the station was used by Nitrovit bulk grain wagons in the 1970s. (M.J.Stretton)

WESTBURY DEPOT

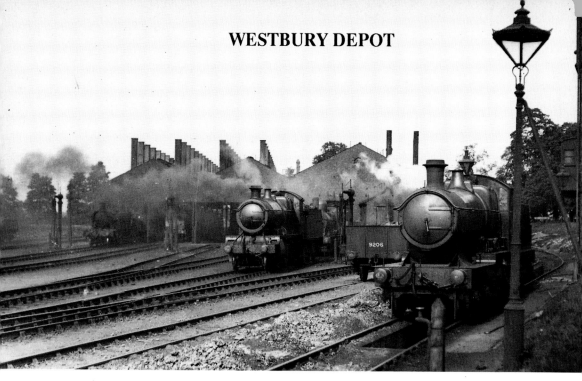

11. The location of the four-road shed is shown south of the station on the 6" scale map. It was opened in 1915 and is seen here on 23rd May 1929, along with nos. 5536, 6307 and 3384. (H.C.Casserley)

12. Taking a few paces backwards, the photographer recorded no. 3550 and wagons on the incline to the coal stage seen on the right of the previous picture. The locomotive was built as a broad gauge convertible 0-4-2ST, rebuilt as an 0-4-4T and then changed to standard gauge as a 4-4-0. (H.C.Casserley)

13. No. 6338 is on the turntable which was east of the shed. This closed in September 1965, a diesel depot being established west of the station. There was a well equipped workshop adjacent to the running shed. (Wessex coll.)

Other views of this station can be found in the companion album *Salisbury to Westbury*.

14. Three sidings were used for the stabling and fuelling of diesel locomotives; DMUs were fuelled here from 1959 onwards. The tracks were extended in 1976. In World War II, ambulance trains were kept on the site. The depot was photographed on 24th February 1991 and was closed on 1st March 1993. No. 33113 is nearest the camera and no. 33111 is behind it. (M.J.Stretton)

15. "Bulldog" class 4-4-0 no. 3412 approaches the station on 27th May 1935. Its train is on the 1848 line from Trowbridge; on the right is the 1900 route from Patney & Chirton, which formed the direct link with London. (H.C.Casserley)

16. Crossing the redesigned junction on 10th September 1987 is no. 47625 *City of Truro* with the 08.25 Gloucester to Eastleigh Speedlink service. The locomotive was renamed *Resplendent* in the following month. The security railings on the right protect the new signal box. The siding on the left had been a loop during World War II. (T.Heavyside)

17. Westbury Power Box is in the background as no. 47490 proceeds towards Hawkeridge Junction with the 11.10 from Portsmouth Harbour on 15th April 1988. The signalling allows for bidirectional running through the three remaining platforms and both freight reception lines. (P.G.Barnes)

18. Following the Southampton - Portsmouth electrification in May 1990, the former Salisbury - Portsmouth DEMU stopping service was discontinued and replaced in part by a new Bristol - Southampton all-stations diagram. This brought DEMUs to Bristol on a daily basis for the first time since 1977 and, on 26th September 1990, one of the eight surviving class 207 units, no. 207013, arrived at Westbury forming the 11.48 Bristol - Southampton. The new "44" headcode replaced the "85" previously allocated to this route. (G.Gillham)

HAWKERIDGE JUNCTION

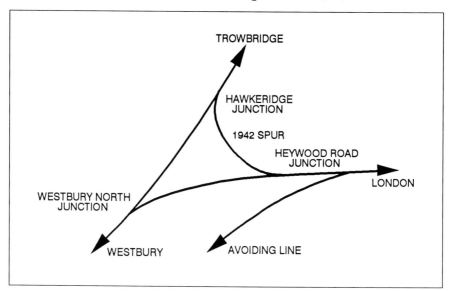

A double track spur between the Trowbridge and Patney & Chirton lines was opened on 14th July 1942 as a diversionary route for wartime traffic. It reduced the need for trains to reverse at Westbury or use the steeply graded line via Devizes. The chord was later used by locomotives on a circular test run from Swindon Works. Known as the Hawkeridge Loop, it became the Westbury East Loop in 1984.

19. Following the opening by Mobil Oil Ltd of a depot in the former goods yard at Frome in 1974, block trains of bitumen tanks became a common sight on the Bath - Westbury line for a period in 1979-80. These were often worked by a pair of class 25 locomotives; nos. 25285 and 25300 pass Hawkeridge Junction with a lengthy load from Ellesmere Port to Frome on 3rd April 1980. This traffic ceased early in 1993. (G.Gillham)

20. During the closure of Westbury station for engineering works in May 1984, a DMU shuttle service was provided between Bristol and Trowbridge with bus connections onwards. The train had to run almost into Westbury to reach the nearest crossover, as recorded on 9th May 1984. The signal box closed five days later. From 1942 until 1950 it controlled access to Government sidings west of the Trowbridge line. Further north, Yarnbrook Box was in use until 6th November 1955. (C.Hall)

21. The junction points were renewed over two Sundays, 23rd and 30th June 1991, the junction itself being moved slightly nearer to Westbury. The new points had been preassembled at the site over the previous three weeks. On Sunday 23rd June the old pointwork is being removed prior to replacement with plain line for one week, although the entry points for the East Chord remained in situ. No. 37207 (the former *William Cookworthy*) is at the head of a materials train and, in the background, no. 37254 is waiting with a ballast train. (S.McMullin)

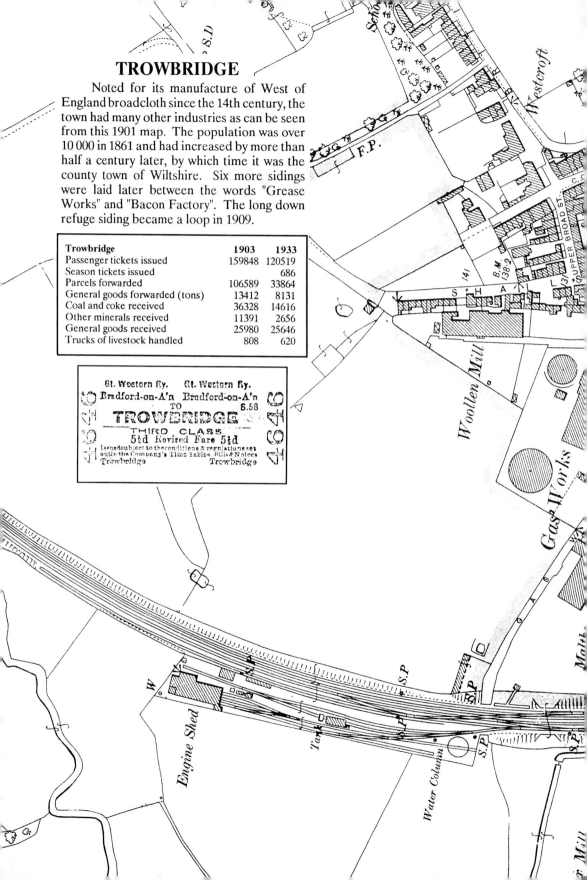

TROWBRIDGE

Noted for its manufacture of West of England broadcloth since the 14th century, the town had many other industries as can be seen from this 1901 map. The population was over 10 000 in 1861 and had increased by more than half a century later, by which time it was the county town of Wiltshire. Six more sidings were laid later between the words "Grease Works" and "Bacon Factory". The long down refuge siding became a loop in 1909.

Trowbridge	1903	1933
Passenger tickets issued	159848	120519
Season tickets issued		686
Parcels forwarded	106589	33864
General goods forwarded (tons)	13412	8131
Coal and coke received	36328	14616
Other minerals received	11391	2656
General goods received	25980	25646
Trucks of livestock handled	808	620

Gt. Western Ry.   Gt. Western Ry.
Bradford-on-A'n Bradford-on-A'n
TO   S.58
TROWBRIDGE
THIRD CLASS
5½d Revised Fare 5½d
Issued subject to the conditions & regulations set out in the Company's Time Tables, Bills & Notices
Trowbridge   Trowbridge

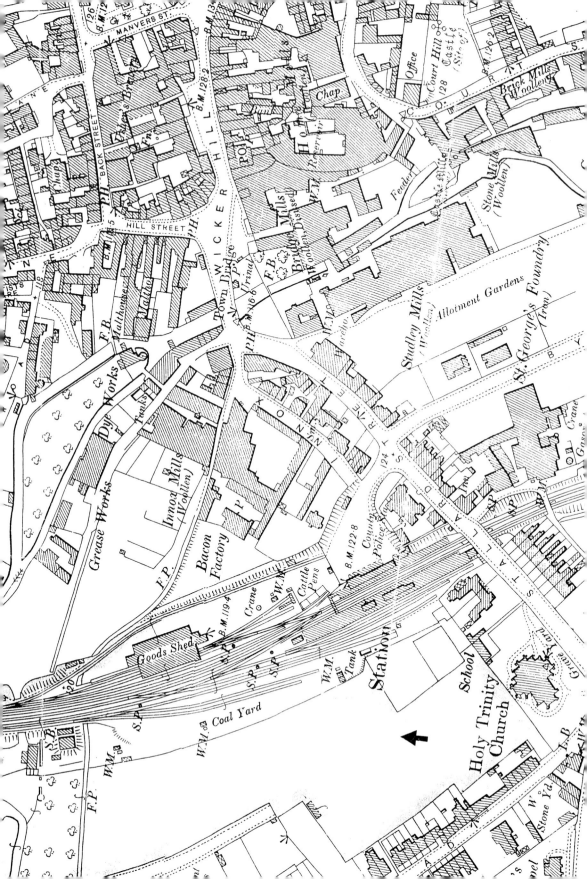

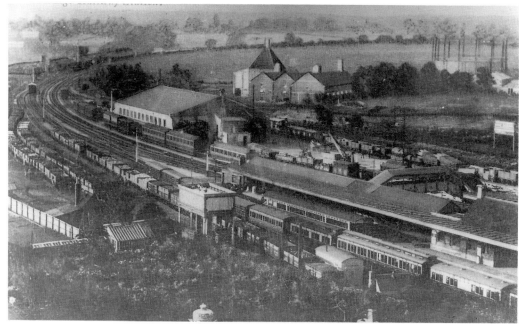

22. A postcard of indifferent quality gives an impression of the extent of this once important station. Look for the autocoach with a tender locomotive attached, the double track doorway to the goods shed and the 8-ton capacity goods yard crane. "Minerals forwarded" (presumably local stone) were listed as 657 tons in 1903, 1364 in 1913, 1137 in 1923 and 2947 in 1937. The engine shed is just visible in the left background. (Lens of Sutton)

23. The engine shed was built in 1875 and contained three 100ft long roads. By 1901, there were 26 locomotives based here but its importance declined after Westbury shed opened in 1915. Closure took place on 2nd June 1923, after which time the building was used for carriage and wagon repairs. The photograph dates from September 1921. (K.Robertson coll.)

24. The lean-to building on the left was the fitting shop. A sand furnace, smithy and stores building were also provided. An additional siding for locomotive coal had been added in about 1910. The turntable was 41ft 8ins in length. (W.A.Camwell)

25. Initially the station was simply an intermediate one when the branch to Westbury from Chippenham opened on 5th September 1848. It later assumed junction status. Diesel and petrol fumes have replaced the stench of horse droppings in most station approach roads. (Lens of Sutton)

26. Autocoach working was commonly employed on the services from here to Devizes, to Chippenham and to Radstock via Camerton, although steam railmotors were often used in 1905-22. The first footbridge was at the far end of the buildings. (Lens of Sutton)

27. A southward view from the footbridge in 1921 shows the generous provision of canopies. The road bridge was rebuilt and the platforms extended thereunder in 1931-32. (H.C.Casserley coll.)

28. The platform lengthening is evident as the classic GWR formation of pannier tank and autocoach was recorded, albeit after the formation of BR. This was designated the down platform but is now the up, the line descriptions between Hawkeridge and Bradford Junctions being reversed on 11th May 1984. (R.S.Carpenter coll.)

29. The end of the platform was visible as no. 8479 was photographed while shunting on 9th April 1955. Other items from the past include the shunters wagon and the sign *TELE-GRAMS*, a service once available at most stations. (L.W.Rowe)

31. No. 4909 *Blakesley Hall* runs in with the 10.10am (Sunday only) Reading to Westbury via Devizes. The dock on the right had end loading facilities. Goods traffic ceased on 10th July 1967. (H.C.Casserley)

30. The up bay is on the right, its track having an engine release crossover until July 1955. The engine turntable was nearby in the early 1880s. This photograph from October 1962 includes the starting signal for up trains leaving from the down platform. The post also carries a route indicator for backing trains. (C.L.Caddy)

32. The 16.15 Cardiff to Portsmouth Harbour was hauled by no. 33024 on 20th August 1981. The class 33s worked these services from May 1980 to May 1988. Canopy reduction had taken place but most buildings were still in situ. (D.Mitchell)

33. The signal box closed on 8th September 1968 and all points were rendered inoperable. Platform reduction had been executed by the time that no. 50001 *Dreadnought* was recorded on 3rd April 1983, while working the 13.25 Sunday service from Paddington to Plymouth. It had been diverted via Chippenham and Melksham. (G.Gillham)

34. The historic buildings were deemed unsafe and were demolished in 1984. The new structure is seen taking shape on 12th June 1988, as DMU nos. C983 and C851 run "wrong-line" owing to engineering work on the up track. They form the 09.00 Bristol to Weymouth train. (S.McMullin)

35. Relaying and reballasting took place near Trowbridge on 12th August 1990, no. 50032 *Courageous* providing the power for one of the trains. The class 50s were then in terminal decline, this example being cut up on 26th March 1991. (S.McMullin)

36. The new building was erected on the opposite side of the track from its predecessor and was photographed on 17th August 1993, as the 12.22 Swansea to Portsmouth Harbour was about to depart at 14.51. The class 158 Super Sprinters brought a new level of comfort to the route. (J.Scrace)

37. The basic class 150 Sprinters help to provide a frequent service to Bath and Bristol which is well used at this station. No. 150421 is working the 13.33 Bristol Temple Meads to Southampton Central on 24th November 1994, a dismal grey day. Minimal shelter is available for passengers. (M.J.Stretton)

BRADFORD JUNCTIONS

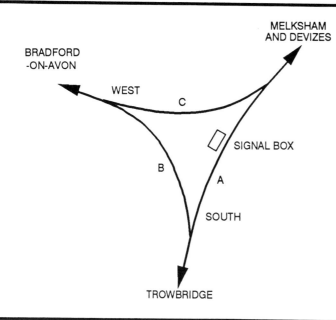

A. Opened 5th September 1848. Closed to regular passenger trains on 18th April 1966 and reopened on 13th May 1985. Singled on 11th March 1990.

B. Opened 2nd February 1857.

C. Opened 10th March 1893. Singled on 26th February 1967. Closed completely in 1990.

From 1893 there was a signal box at each junction but this was replaced by the one marked, on 2nd May 1933. It controlled motorised points.

38. After local passenger services were withdrawn on 6th May 1968, the Chippenham to Bradford Junction route was retained for freight traffic and as a diversionary route for passenger trains during weekend engineering work on the Bristol or West of England main lines. However, after pressure from local councils and other interested groups, BR agreed to reopen Melksham station and initiate a limited Swindon - Westbury local service in May 1985. Class 119 DMU set L575 passes Bradford Junction working the 13.30 (Saturdays only) Swindon - Westbury on 25th January 1986. At this time Bradford Junction signal box (left background) was the last outpost of mechanical semaphore signalling in Wiltshire. (G.Gillham)

39. No. 59002 *Yeoman Enterprise* heads the 10.10 Wootton Bassett to Merehead Quarry empties on 7th March 1990 and traverses the temporary way laid prior to the removal of the up line a few days later. (S.McMullin)

40. The old pointwork is being removed on 11th March 1990, while no. 47327 waits with a train loaded with track panels. Also visible is Bradford Junction box which closed six days later when its work was transferred to Westbury. (S.McMullin)

EAST OF
BRADFORD-ON-AVON

41. The route first crosses the River Avon west of Bradford West Junction and passes over it for the second time on this skew bridge on the approach to the station. Another bridge nearby spans the water from the weir. No. 33010 is working the 09.50 Swansea to Portsmouth Harbour on 5th April 1988. (J.Scrace)

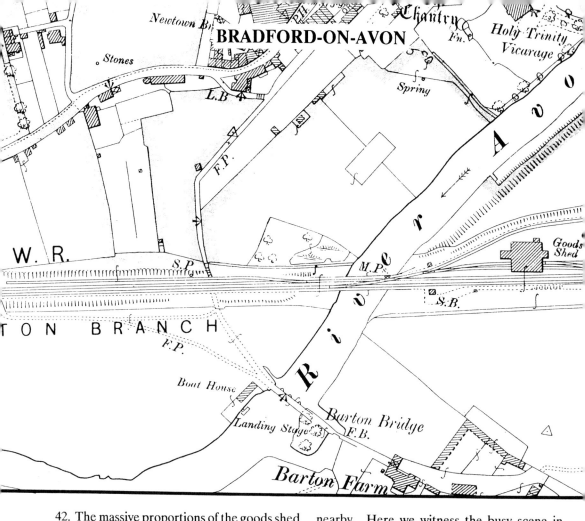

BRADFORD-ON-AVON

42. The massive proportions of the goods shed reflect the importance of this traffic at this location. The crane was of 6-ton capacity. This is another old-established town for wool products; it also had important stone quarries nearby. Here we witness the busy scene in 1926. Tonnage of minerals despatched was recorded as 3604 in 1903, 1050 in 1913, 1269 in 1923 and 694 in 1933. (H.C.Casserley)

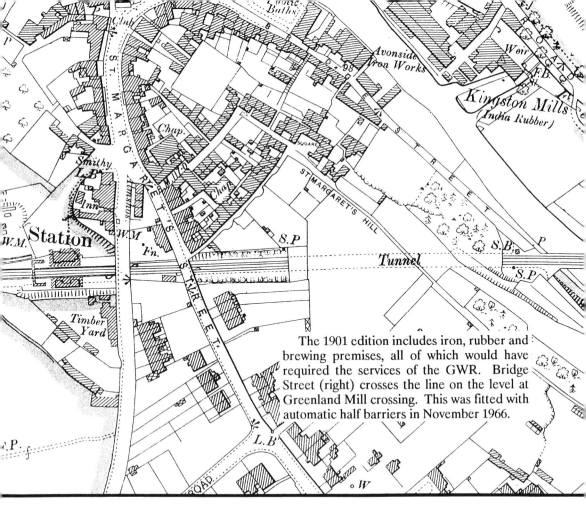

The 1901 edition includes iron, rubber and brewing premises, all of which would have required the services of the GWR. Bridge Street (right) crosses the line on the level at Greenland Mill crossing. This was fitted with automatic half barriers in November 1966.

43. As at Trowbridge, the goods shed had doorways to accommodate two tracks. No. 3223 poses by the cabbages growing on the staff allotments on 25th September 1926. It was a member of the "Barnum" class. (H.C.Casserley)

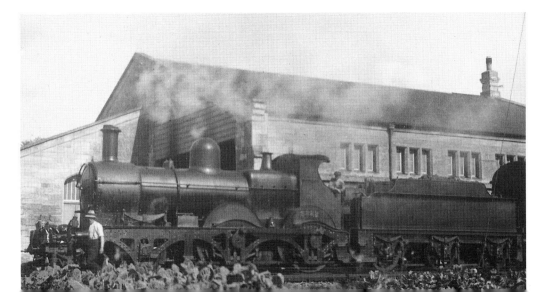

44. The station was built no less than ten years before the railway opened and was intended to be a terminus of a branch from Staverton. This is a westward view in the 1930s, when some minor work was taking place. (Mowat coll.)

45. A "Hall" class 4-6-0 bursts into the station as it speeds west with an express in August 1962. Local stone was used for much of the old town and also for most of the lineside structures. (A.J.Pike/F.Hornby)

Bradford-on-Avon	1903	1933
Passenger tickets issued	69651	72529
Season tickets issued		833
Parcels forwarded	20312	42408
General goods forwarded (tons)	2045	2556
Coal and coke received	8044	3330
Other minerals received	5497	2906
General goods received	5119	4814
Trucks of livestock handled	39	1

46. The high ground in the distance was penetrated by the 159yd long Bradford Tunnel, visible through the footbridge in this June 1963 view. Also evident is part of the goods yard which closed to general traffic on 2nd November 1964 but remained in use for coal for a further 12 months. (C.L.Caddy)

47. No. 33062 passes under the roofless and partially painted footbridge on 20th August 1981, as it hauls the 15.10 Portsmouth Harbour to Bristol Temple Meads. Bull head meets flat bottom rail here. (D.Mitchell)

48. No. 50002 speeds through with a diverted south west-north east service on 10th May 1986. The rear part of the train is on the down gradient of 1 in 115 while the front is level. (P.G.Barnes)

49. With slit windows, projecting canopies and a squat form, the station gave a solid, everlasting appearance in 1993. Long may it serve a useful purpose in this historic town, which (unlike Trowbridge) had a drop in population from 8032 in 1861 to 5760 in 1961. This was partly attributable to boundary changes however. (J.Scrace)

50. Emerging from Bradford Tunnel and passing under the two road bridges is Sprinter no. 150221, running as the 12.33 Southampton Central to Bristol Temple Meads. Few stations retained so much of their early structure. (M.J.Stretton)

WEST OF
BRADFORD-ON-AVON

51. Viewed from the stone bridge featured on the cover of this album, no. 47533 crosses the 77yd long Bradford Viaduct over the River Avon on 25th April 1988, with the 11.10 Portsmouth Harbour to Cardiff. Sprinters were soon to takeover these services. (D.Mitchell)

The Kennet & Avon Canal is at the top of this 1901 map and is shown to pass over both the GWR and the River Avon. The Westwood Quarry Tramway has wharfage on both the railway and the canal. The standard gauge private siding was in use periodically until 1936, although the connection at its western end was removed in 1905.

Stone

AVONCLIFF

421 1.752

T & A V O N C A N A L

424 1.748 Crane

Stone Yard
Crane

S.E. & P.

NCH

Aqueduct

A v o n

Bradford on Avon
Union Workhouse

L.B

Avon Villa

Stone Gate

Crane

Avon Cottage

T R A M W A Y

Avo

F.P.

F.B.

F.P.

W

Spring

W

Quarry

F.P.

W

L.B

Well House

Uppe

52. This westward view features the halt which was built on the east side of the twin-arch canal bridge and opened on 9th July 1906. It was intended for use by autocoach or railmotor operated trains. (Lens of Sutton)

53. A 1963 photograph includes the occupation crossing which was not for use by passengers. They were expected to use the canal bridge, an unusual means of platform connection. (C.L.Caddy)

54. A pleasure boat uses the aqueduct in 1986. The canal was acquired by the GWR in 1852 who fixed exhorbitant tolls to discourage its use. Decline and closure followed. (P.G.Barnes)

55. No seats or shelters were available on 25th April 1988 when no. 33006 was pictured with the 10.10 Portsmouth Harbour to Swansea. Locomotive hauled trains seldom stopped here at that time. (D.Mitchell)

56. A rare example of a BR station restored to GWR style. No. 158870 speeds through on 24th November 1994 working the 11.24 Portsmouth Harbour to Cardiff, then inexplicably termed an "Alphaline" service. Selected trains called by request, most being on Weymouth journeys. (M.J.Stretton)

WEST OF AVONCLIFF

57. Freshford is in the background as a class 47 takes a Bristol-Weymouth train round one of the many curves on this part of the route on 2nd April 1988. The Kennet & Avon Canal (right) and the River Avon take a similar course and add to the beauty of the region. Freshford Viaduct is right of centre and is 114yds long. (P.G.Barnes)

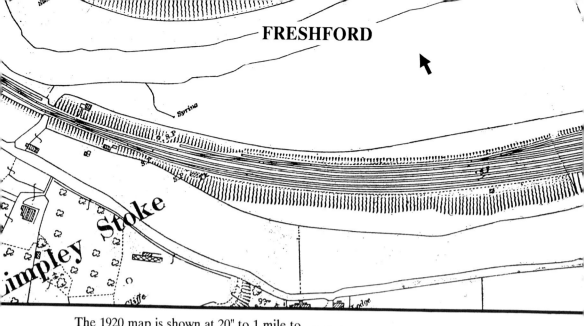

The 1920 map is shown at 20" to 1 mile to include the goods loops and exchange sidings that were laid down in 1910 between Freshford (right) and Limpley Stoke (left) in connection with the opening of the Camerton line. Also on the left is Limpley Stoke South Box which was in use until 24th August 1969, although the suffix "South" had been dropped in 1927.

Freshford	1903	1933
Passenger tickets issued	19927	15450
Season tickets issued		97
Parcels forwarded	2987	2505
General goods forwarded (tons)	144	162
Coal and coke received	105	320
Other minerals received	247	48
General goods received	274	509
Trucks of livestock handled	-	-

58.   There were no goods facilities at Freshford until 1910 when the short siding (left of centre) was provided. It is unusual to find painters in a staff group photograph such as this. (Lens of Sutton)

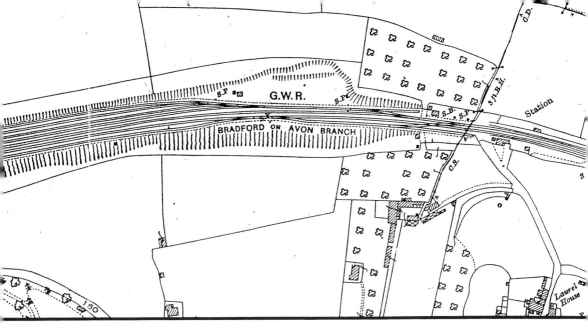

59. Looking towards Limpley Stoke we see (from left to right) the down siding, down goods loop, down main, up main, up goods loop, and three exchange sidings. It is evident that wagons were stored therein but their main purpose was for coal wagons to and from the collieries on the Camerton branch. Many were destined for Southampton in trains of up to 60 wagons. (Mowat coll.)

60. Dainty canopies, well kept flower beds and the obligatory fire buckets are features of this photograph from the 1930s that are now things of the past. There was an occupation crossing between the signal box and the buffer stops. (Mowat coll.)

61. The down home signals had to be sited at the end of the advertisement-prone up platform owing to the curvature of the track. The lower arm was for the goods loop. (H.C.Casserley coll.)

62. "Bulldog" class 4-4-0 no. 3446 *Goldfinch* retards the 3.52pm Westbury to Bristol on 9th June 1930. Stopping at all stations, it was due at Temple Meads at 5.2pm. (H.C.Casserley)

63. Photographed on 2nd June 1963, the signal box was taken out of use on 18th August 1963, along with the sidings and loops. Goods services had been curtailed on 10th June of that year. (C.L.Caddy)

64. The 16.18 Bristol to Weymouth stopping train slows to call at Freshford on 10th May 1986. At this period, only two other up trains stopped here - the 17.18 and 17.45 from Temple Meads. (P.G.Barnes)

65. The same service is seen accelerating gently away from its stop on 5th April 1988. The line curves left in the distance and crossed the old Somerset/Wiltshire border at the Avon Viaduct. (D.Mitchell)

66. A travelling percussionist appears to have jettisoned his equipment prior to unit 158863 passing through as the 12.30 Cardiff to Portsmouth Harbour on 17th August 1993. (J.Scrace)

67. Winding its way down the well wooded valley on 17th August 1993 is no. 59001 *Yeoman Endeavour* with the 11.52 stone train from Merehead Quarry to Hallen Marsh. The material was required for the second Severn crossing project. The train is climbing at 1 in 242 on this curve. (J.Scrace)

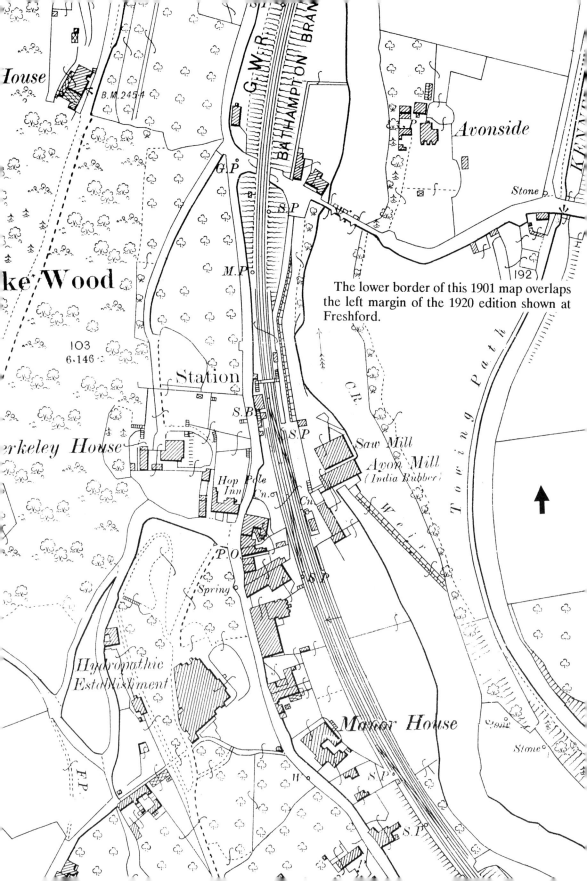

The lower border of this 1901 map overlaps
the left margin of the 1920 edition shown at
Freshford.

68. Blocks of Bath stone from the nearby mine await loading at the down siding, while empty wagons stand near the goods shed. Cranes were provided on both sides. In 1903, 2736 tons of stone were despatched. In 1913 the figure was 577 but in most years thereafter it was under 100. This signal box was superseded in 1910 by two others. (K.Robertson coll.)

69. The Camerton line was completed to Limpley Stoke on 9th May 1910 and a small bay platform was added at the north end of the down platform. It is to the left of the down starting signals in this 1921 view. (H.C.Casserley coll.)

70. A closer look reveals that the platforms were of timber construction owing to their location on an embankment. The bay platform also extends across the road bridge. Passenger trains to Camerton and beyond were run until 22nd March 1915 and again between 8th July 1923 and 21st September 1925. (Mowat coll.)

71. A southward view from the 1930s includes the saw and rubber mills along with the 1910 North Box. This was demoted to a ground frame on 5th September 1927, when it lost its description "North". This and the previous picture were taken in the 1930s. (Mowat coll.)

Limpley Stoke	1903	1933
Passenger tickets issued	25695	13239
Season tickets issued		136
Parcels forwarded	3088	1912
General goods forwarded (tons)	901	867
Coal and coke received	399	196
Other minerals received	937	10
General goods received	787	137
Trucks of livestock handled	-	7

72. Wind swirls the steam to spoil the photograph of no. 4574 arriving with an up train on 9th June 1930. However, the picture does show clearly the connection to the Camerton line which ran parallel to the main line for half a mile. The branch was closed to freight traffic on 15th February 1951. (H.C.Casserley coll.)

73. The last steam locomotive to be built by BR, class 9F 2-10-0 no. 92220 *Evening Star*, runs south on 15th July 1960 with a Cardiff to Portsmouth train. By then there was no trace of the Camerton tracks, but old-style name-board lettering was in use. (T.Wright)

74. The signal box that closed in 1910 was retained as an office and was still to be seen on 2nd June 1963 as the 14.00 Bristol Temple Meads to Weymouth DMU passed by the site of the sidings. In its final years, the station was designated a halt. Camping coaches were to be found here in many summers during the 1950s. (C.L.Caddy)

75. When photographed on 2nd June 1963, barriers were up to prevent passengers using the timber parts of the platforms. Freight services had been withdrawn on 4th January 1960 and complete closure followed on 3rd October 1966. (C.L.Caddy)

76. Staffing had ceased on 1st March 1961. The signal box could be used to move the Camerton branch points until track removal was completed in December 1958. The branch had been used for the filming of the "Titfield Thunderbolt" in 1952. (A.J.Pike/F.Hornby)

77. A class 33 passes the sole remaining building, southbound on 10th May 1986. In 1995 the structure was occupied by a transport bookseller trading under the name of "Titfield Thunderbolt". (P.G.Barnes)

SOUTH OF BATHAMPTON

78. About one mile north of Limpley Stoke, the Kennet & Avon Canal passes over the River Avon and the railway again, this time on Dundas Aqueduct. Sprinter no. 155315 is seen north thereof on 2nd February 1990, working the 09.16 Cardiff to Portsmouth Harbour "wrong line". This was due to closure of the up line following flood damage to the embankment. Most freight trains were diverted until repairs were completed in October. (S.McMullin)

79.   The typical five-coach formation of a Portsmouth Harbour-Cardiff service was recorded in the scenic north end of the valley on 8th November 1986, a class 33 leading. The Kennet & Avon Canal (foreground) was fully reopened on 8th August 1990 and transport history was made in 1994 when stone was conveyed by barge again from Limpley Stoke. A batch was moved to Windsor for castle repairs. (T.Heavyside)

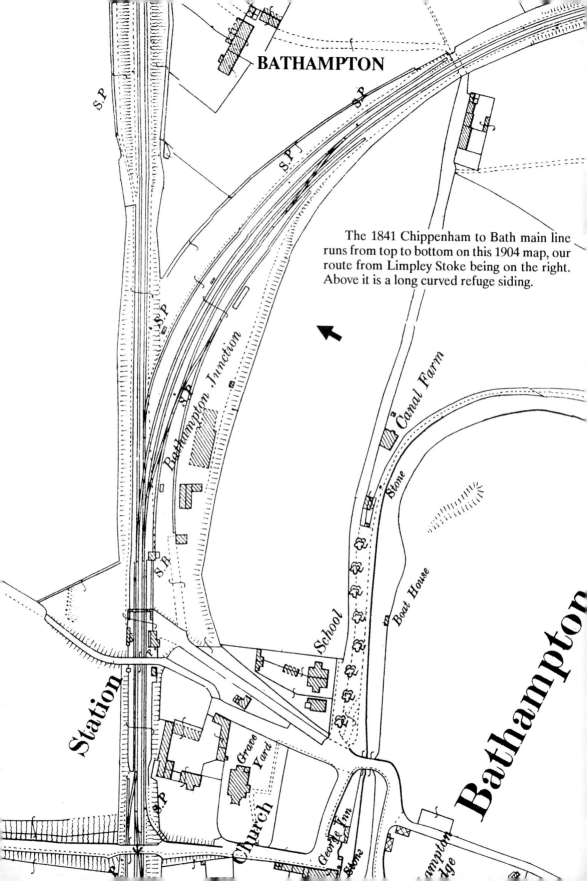

BATHAMPTON

The 1841 Chippenham to Bath main line runs from top to bottom on this 1904 map, our route from Limpley Stoke being on the right. Above it is a long curved refuge siding.

Bathampton Junction

Canal Farm

Stone

Boat House

School

Station

Grave Yard

Church

George Inn

Bathampton

Bathampton.

80. A north facing postcard view features the footbridge at the end of the station approach road. It was taken from the canal bridge which is lower right on the map. (C.G.Maggs coll.)

Bathampton	1903	1933
Passenger tickets issued	35117	16801
Season tickets issued		259
Parcels forwarded	3243	1599
General goods forwarded (tons)	758	961
Coal and coke received	181	264
Other minerals received	730	150
General goods received	2950	2167
Trucks of livestock handled	3	-

81. This and the next three photographs were taken in about 1908. The 1.10pm from Paddington was hauled by 4-4-2T no. 2225 according to notes on the reverse of the picture. It was one of the "County Tank" class. (J.S.Heap/H.Tasker)

82. A down express approaches the junction, the signal having its lamps well below the arms. To the right of the multi-insulatored telegraph post is the down refuge siding.
(J.S.Heap/H.Tasker)

83. Track workers lean on their tools as a train bound for the South Coast complies with the 25mph restriction on the curve east of the junction. The refuge siding is seen again.
(J.S.Heap/H.Tasker)

84. Sadly the details of the "County" class locomotive and its destination were not recorded but the train is leaving the main line for the Westbury route. The siding in the foreground retains bridge rails and longitudinal timbers of the type used on broad gauge track.
(J.S.Heap/H.Tasker)

85. Wide platforms and a covered footbridge were provided for crowds that seldom appeared, although some passengers would have changed trains here. (Mowat coll.)

86. An early example of electric welding using a portable generator was recorded in the goods yard in about 1930. The yard seems to have also been used to accommodate sleepers and bridge girders. Stacks of chairs appear in picture no. 81. (C.G.Maggs coll.)

87. SR class U 2-6-0 no. 1624 eases its Portsmouth-Bristol train onto the main line on 19th September 1936. The SR and GWR worked the through service beyond Salisbury together. Note the ornamented roof valance. (H.C.Casserley)

88. A "Castle" 4-6-0 rumbles over the junction pointwork as it speeds towards Bath from London in about 1937. The crane on the right was not listed as being available for public goods traffic. (R.S.Carpenter coll.)

89. A view from the bridge marked at the bottom of the map includes the down starting signal and the points of the up refuge siding. This was converted into a loop to speed wartime traffic on 1st November 1942. (H.C.Casserley coll.)

90. An up express passes through in August 1962 hauled by "Hall" class 4-6-0 no. 7903 *Foremarke Hall* as we gain a glimpse of the down loop points. This loop was in use from 1st November 1942 until 17th August 1970. (A.J.Pike/F.Hornby)

91. A new signal box came into use on 21st September 1956, but it had a short life, closing on 17th August 1970. This and the next picture were taken in September 1964, the goods yard having closed on 10th June 1963. (C.L.Caddy)

92. Station staffing ceased on 4th January 1965 and trains stopped calling after 3rd October 1966. A concrete span had replaced the steel of the previous bridge. The reason for the low position of the up starting signals is evident. The station was officially a halt in its last years. (C.L.Caddy)

93. New pointwork was assembled in the former goods yard and the track alterations were recorded on 2nd February 1986. The new points and large radius curves resulted in the speed limit being raised to 40 mph. The occupation bridge from which this picture was taken was demolished in February 1995 as part of the Bathampton bypass project. (S.McMullin)

94. The improved track resulted in down trains joining the main line west of the bridge last seen in picture no. 92. No. 33064 is about to do so on 26th March 1988 while working the 11.10 Portsmouth Harbour to Cardiff service. (P.G.Barnes)

95. Turning round and looking over the other side of the bridge, six weeks later, we witness no. 3302, with the 08.00 Cardiff to Portsmouth Harbour, overtaking no. 47634 *Henry Ford*, which is standing on the up goods loop with Chipman's weed control train. (S.McMullin)

96. The west end of the new crossover is seen here as no. 156472 is about to use it to reach the Westbury up line on 15th April 1989, while working the 10.35 Cardiff to Portsmouth Harbour. Note the new signal gantry - the one seen in the previous view was in use only briefly, from February 1986 until April 1989. (S.McMullin)

97. Running on mixed gauge track, a broad gauge train runs under the bridge seen in the background of the previous picture. The timbers under the rails were originally supported each end on wooden piles. (C.G.Maggs coll.)

98. Candy's bridge is featured as a westbound HST from Paddington runs past the signal for the up goods loop on 26th March 1988. These trains have brought the best service ever between London, Bath and Bristol. (P.G.Barnes)

99. Regular locomotive-hauled passenger services on the Bristol-Portsmouth route ceased in May 1973, and for the next four years were replaced by "Hampshire" DEMUs, usually in pairs. Units 1127 and 1128 are seen nearing Bathampton, on 28th March 1977 forming the 11.15 Bristol-Portsmouth service. Two months later these units were replaced, again by locomotive haulage, in the form of ex-Midland Region Class 31s. (G.Gillham)

EAST OF BATH

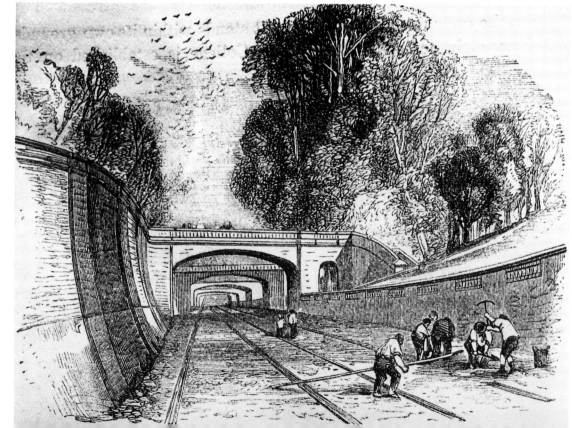

100. Hampton Row signal box was situated one mile east of Bath and was in use from 19th July 1904 until 3rd April 1910. A halt opened on the same day as the box but was in use only until 29th April 1917. A down train was photographed, in about 1908, approaching the platforms which are just out of the picture. (J.S.Heap/H.Tasker)

101. An engraving from about 1852 illustrates some of the ornamental stonework required where the broad gauge tracks cut through the beautiful Sydney Gardens on the approach to the city. (C.G.Maggs coll.)

102. A temporary platform was built in 1889 for the arrival of Princess Helen for a special event in Sydney Gardens. Note the dual gauge track; broad gauge working ceased in 1892, the third rail having been laid in 1874. (C.G.Maggs coll.)

103.   Rebuilt "Star" class no. 4032 *Queen Alexandra* runs through Sydney Gardens on the down line sometime in the late 1930s. The appealing Bath stone became encrusted with soot in this vicinity. The wall here supports the Kennet & Avon Canal. (R.S.Carpenter coll.)

105.   The 16.10 Bristol to Brighton rumbles over the River Avon on 31st May 1985, hauled by a class 33 diesel. It is about to traverse the 255yd long Dolemeads Viaduct, east of the station. (J.Scrace)

104.   Watched by one man and his dog, class 117 DMU no. B427 passes through Sydney Gardens, forming the 13.05 Weymouth-Bristol on 21st June 1983. The elimination of rail joints has brought more peace to the gardens. The tunnels are 77 and 99 yds in length. (G.Gillham)

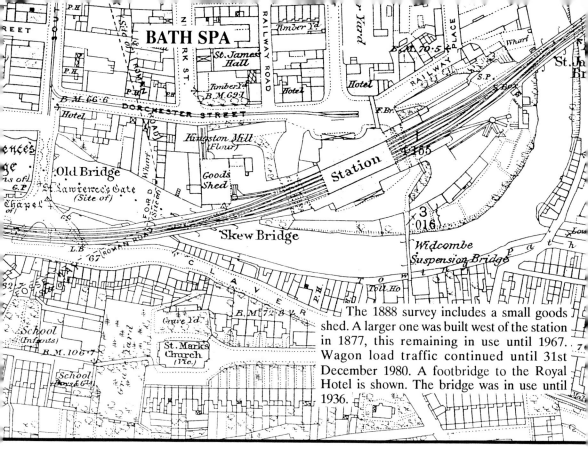

106. Although of poor quality, this photograph (looking north in the 1850s) shows the roof that covered all four tracks until 1897.

The bridge over the Avon is on the right and Bath Abbey is in the left background. (C.G.Maggs coll.)

The 1888 survey includes a small goods shed. A larger one was built west of the station in 1877, this remaining in use until 1967. Wagon load traffic continued until 31st December 1980. A footbridge to the Royal Hotel is shown. The bridge was in use until 1936.

107. The Bath stone north elevation was photographed in about 1886, along with samples of road transport of the era. Horse power also served the tramway. (C.G.Maggs coll.)

108. An eastward panorama from about 1895 includes the overall roof and the old goods shed to the left of the nearest end of it. A small shed for locomotives had been provided beyond it in the early years. (C.G.Maggs coll.)

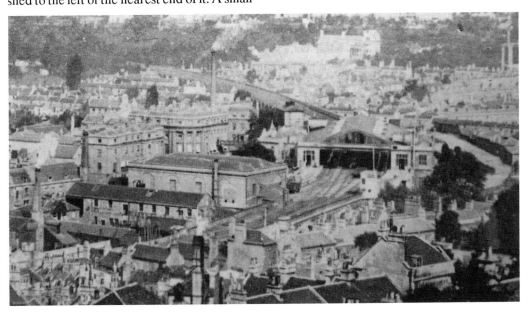

109. Platform canopies of great length were constructed during the 1897 rebuilding, as can be seen in this view from about 1905. The station was sited close to the city centre. (C.G.Maggs coll.)

110. The south elevation was recorded in about 1925, along with contemporary road transport. There were separate subways for passengers, luggage, pedestrians and carriages. (British Rail)

111. A high level signal box replaced the two that were situated at opposite ends of the station until 1897. The box is seen in the 1930s along with the point to the electricity works siding which was horse worked into the 1950s. Track circuiting was introduced here in 1914. (Mowat coll.)

112. A wagon turntable was used to serve three short sidings at the east end of the down platform until January 1960. The connection (between the locomotives) to the centre roads was removed in 1962 and the southern one was taken out of use. (K.Robertson coll.)

113. This small shed was provided in the goods yard west of the station and was in use until February 1961. 2-6-2T no. 5528 was pictured in residence in 1949. (H.C.Casserley coll.)

114. Generations of railway managers have taken advantage of Bath's architectural joys to promote rail travel to the historic city where the Romans established the baths. (British Rail)

BATH - *The Georgian City*

INFORMATION FROM SPA DIRECTOR, THE PUMP ROOM, BATH

TRAVEL BY TRAIN   BRITISH RAILWAYS

115. The original goods yard sidings (latterly used by the electricity works) were finally removed in 1960 to allow this extension of the up platform to be undertaken, so that long trains did not have to draw up and stop a second time. (Lens of Sutton)

Gt. Western Ry.   Gt. Western Ry.

Trowbridge   Trowbridge

TO

WARMINSTER

11d, THIRD CLASS 11d,

Issued subject to the conditions & regulations set out in the Company's Time Tables Books and Bills.   (H.G)

Warminster   Warminster

OCT.26 92

3404

116. The 4.33pm Salisbury to Bristol Temple Meads formed of five ex-SR coaches stands behind no. 6918 *Sandon Hall* in July 1963. It called at all stations to Bath Spa, arriving at 6.1pm. (A.J.Pike/F.Hornby)

117. The up bay (right) and the remaining usable centre road (right) were both taken out of use on 31st March 1967. The elevated signal box was functioning until 21st January 1968. (Lens of Sutton)

118. On the cold, damp evening of Sunday 3rd January 1982, no. 47030 stands with the 16.20 Paddington-Bristol. The wisps of steam from around the loco and coaches show that the train is steam heated - probably one of the last on this route to be so, as steam heating was abolished soon afterwards. (G.Gillham)

Bath's other station - Green Park - is featured in our *Bath to Evercreech Junction* album.

120.   Alphaline Super Sprinter no. 158866 runs past that part of the platform which was destroyed by an enemy bomb on 27th April 1942. It is seen on 24th November 1994, having left Brighton at 09.00. The electronic destination indicator shows "Aberdaugleddau" - a few seconds later it would change to Milford Haven, one of an increasing number of destinations available on the improved services from this important station. (J.M.Stretton)

119.   A final look at the combination of five MkI coaches and class 33 that served the route to Portsmouth and Brighton well for so many years. No. 33012 has just passed the vestige of the signal box in the canopy, and the concrete flower tubs on 2nd May 1987. (M.Turvey)

MP Middleton Press

Easebourne Lane, Midhurst. West Sussex. GU29 9AZ   Tel: 01730 813169   Fax: 01730 812601

. . . . . Write or telephone for our latest list . . . . .

BRANCH LINES

Branch Line to Allhallows
Branch Lines to Alton
Branch Lines around Ascot
Branch Line to Bude
Branch Lines to East Grinstead
Branch Lines around Effingham Jn
Branch Lines to Exmouth
Branch Line to Fairford
Branch Line to Hawkhurst
Branch Lines to Horsham
Branch Lines around Huntingdon
Branch Lines to Ilfracombe
Branch Line to Lyme Regis
Branch Line to Lynton
Branch Lines around March
Branch Lines around Midhurst
Branch Lines to Newport
Branch Line to Padstow
Branch Lines around Portmadoc 1923-46
Branch Lines around Porthmadog 1954-94
Branch Lines to Seaton & Sidmouth
Branch Line to Selsey
Branch Lines around Sheerness
Branch Line to Southwold
Branch Line to Swanage
Branch Line to Tenterden
Branch Lines to Torrington
Branch Lines to Tunbridge Wells
Branch Lines around Weymouth

LONDON SUBURBAN RAILWAYS

Caterham and Tattenham Corner
Clapham Jn. to Beckenham Jn.
Crystal Palace and Catford Loop
Holborn Viaduct to Lewisham
London Bridge to Addiscombe
Mitcham Junction Lines
South London Line
West Croydon to Epsom

STEAMING THROUGH

Steaming through Cornwall
Steaming through East Sussex
Steaming through the Isle of Wight
Steaming through Surrey
Steaming through West Hants
Steaming through West Sussex

COUNTRY BOOKS

Brickmaking in Sussex
East Grinstead Then and Now

SOUTH COAST RAILWAYS

Ashford to Dover
Bournemouth to Weymouth
Brighton to Eastbourne
Brighton to Worthing
Chichester to Portsmouth
Dover to Ramsgate
Hastings to Ashford
Ryde to Ventnor
Worthing to Chichester

SOUTHERN MAIN LINES

Bromley South to Rochester
Charing Cross to Orpington
Crawley to Littlehampton
Dartford to Sittingbourne
East Croydon to Three Bridges
Epsom to Horsham
Exeter to Barnstaple
Faversham to Dover
Haywards Heath to Seaford
London Bridge to East Croydon
Orpington to Tonbridge
Sittingbourne to Ramsgate
Swanley to Ashford
Three Bridges to Brighton
Tonbridge to Hastings
Victoria to Bromley South
Waterloo to Windsor
Woking to Southampton
Yeovil to Exeter

COUNTRY RAILWAY ROUTES

Andover to Southampton
Bath to Evercreech Junction
Bournemouth to Evercreech Jn
Burnham to Evercreech Junction
Croydon to East Grinstead
East Kent Light Railway
Fareham to Salisbury
Guildford to Redhill
Porthmadog to Blaenau
Reading to Basingstoke
Reading to Guildford
Redhill to Ashford
Salisbury to Westbury
Strood to Paddock Wood
Westbury to Bath
Woking to Alton

BUS BOOKS

Eastbourne Bus Story
Tillingbourne Bus Story

SOUTHERN RAILWAY VIDEOS

Memories of the Hayling Island Branch
Memories of the Lyme Regis Branch
War on the Line

TRAMWAY CLASSICS

Bournemouth & Poole Tramways
Brighton's Tramways
Camberwell & W. Norwood Tramways
Croydon's Tramways
Dover's Tramways
East Ham & West Ham Tramways
Embankment & Waterloo Tramways
Exeter & Taunton Tramways
Greenwich & Dartford Tramways
Hampstead & Highgate Tramways
Hastings Tramways
Lewisham & Catford Tramways
Maidstone & Chatham Tramways
North Kent Tramways
Southampton Tramways
Southend-on-sea Tramways
Thanet's Tramways
Victoria & Lambeth Tramways

OTHER RAILWAY BOOKS

Garraway Father & Son
Industrial Railways of the South East
London Chatham & Dover Railway
South Eastern Railway
War on the Line

MILITARY BOOKS

Battle Over Sussex 1940
Blitz Over Sussex 1941-42
Bombers over Sussex 1943-45
Military Defence of West Sussex

WATERWAY ALBUMS

Hampshire Waterways
Kent and East Sussex Waterways
London to Portsmouth Waterway
West Sussex Waterways